The Thirteen Colonies

by Susan E. Hamen

Content Consultant
Heather Rampton, M.Ed.
Gilder Lehrman 2011 Nevada History Teacher of the Year
Knudson Middle School, Las Vegas, Nevada

CORE
LIBRARY

Published by ABDO Publishing Company, PO Box 398166, Minneapolis, MN 55439. Copyright © 2013 by Abdo Consulting Group, Inc. International copyrights reserved in all countries. No part of this book may be reproduced in any form without written permission from the publisher. The Core Library™ is a trademark and logo of ABDO Publishing Company.

Printed in the United States of America,
North Mankato, Minnesota
112012
012013

Editor: Blythe Hurley
Series Designer: Becky Daum

Cataloging-in-Publication Data
Hamen, Susan E.
 The thirteen colonies / Susan E. Hamen.
   p. cm. -- (Foundations of our nation)
Includes bibliographical references and index.
ISBN 978-1-61783-712-8
1. United States--History--Colonial period, ca. 1600-1775--Juvenile literature.   I. Title.
973.2--dc22

                                            2012946536

Photo Credits: North Wind/North Wind Picture Archives, cover, 1, 8, 10, 13, 16, 19, 22, 25, 28, 31, 33, 34, 37, 39; AP Images, 4, 14, 45; Red Line Editorial, 7; George Widman/AP Images, 27

Cover: The Boston Harbor was part of one of the 13 colonies.

CONTENTS

CHAPTER ONE

A New World

In approximately 1585, an English lord named Sir Walter Raleigh tried to create the first English settlement in North America. He helped pay for approximately 100 people to sail to Roanoke Island in present-day North Carolina. The settlers would have to build their own communities. The only other people living there were American Indians. What would become of these settlers?

Sir Walter Raleigh is commissioned by Queen Elizabeth I of England to found an American colony in Virginia in 1592.

European settlers crossed the Atlantic Ocean to create a new life for themselves. They built communities called colonies. The story of how the United States of America became a country begins with these 13 colonies.

Crossing the Atlantic

Those wanting to cross the Atlantic in search of a new life had to endure voyages that could last months. Food often began to run out before the ships made it to America. Some people died during these voyages. Those who made it were often hungry and weak. Many suffered from a disease called scurvy, which is caused by a lack of vitamin C.

Raleigh's First Colony

Raleigh's first group of settlers endured harsh living conditions and often fought with the American Indian tribes in the area. Everyone in the colony returned to England with explorer Sir Francis Drake. He had arrived in America ten months after the first settlers.

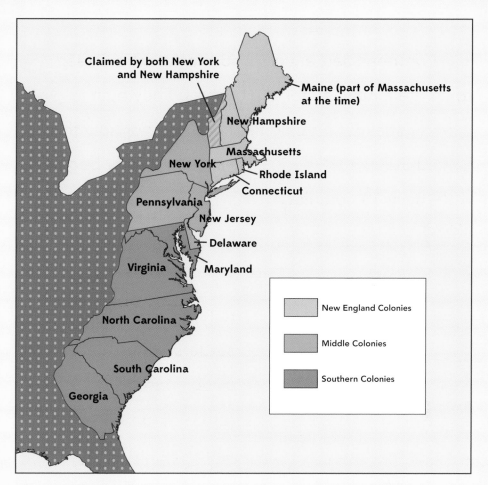

The 13 Colonies before the Revolutionary War

This map shows the original 13 colonies as they looked before the Revolutionary War. What do you notice about the area that is now the state of Maine? Which states have changed since colonial times?

The Lost Colony

The following year, Raleigh tried again to colonize Roanoke Island. Three years later he returned to the island after a long trip to England. All of the colonists

The Roanoke Colony was found abandoned without a trace in 1591, except for the word CROATOAN carved into a tree.

were gone. The only clue they had been there was the word *CROATOAN* carved into a tree at the settlement. Had the settlers gone to a nearby island called Croatoan? Or had there been trouble between the settlers and the Croatoan Indians? The mystery of "The Lost Colony" has never been solved.

The First Colony

King James I granted two companies the right to start colonies in North America. In December 1606, the London Company sent three ships to the Virginia Colony. The 104 men and boys on board established Jamestown Colony in 1607. It was the first permanent English settlement in the first American colony. The Plymouth Company tried to establish a colony in August 1607. It was abandoned after a year.

EXPLORE ONLINE

Imagine you have been chosen to be the governor of a colony in the New World. Your job is to bring a group of colonists across the ocean to begin a new settlement. Go to the Web site below, and take the test to see how well your group would do on their long voyage. What additional information did you learn from the Web site? What information was similar to information in Chapter 1?

Fantastic Voyage
www.pbs.org/wnet/colonialhouse/history/voyage.html

CHAPTER TWO

Jamestown— America's First Settlement

The settlers of Jamestown were adventurous men who believed the New World was rich with gold and other precious metals. They were not prepared for a hard life in the wilderness. Lack of food and clean water caused many to become sick and weak. Approximately half of the settlers died by the end of their first summer.

Tobacco ships docked in the James River during the 1600s. The ships transported the tobacco crop that helped Jamestown Colony become successful.

Captain John Smith and Pocahontas

Captain John Smith was one of the leaders of the Jamestown settlers. He befriended the American Indians and turned to them for help. He traded supplies in exchange for corn. But there was not enough corn to feed the settlers. The people of Jamestown needed to learn how to plant their own crops.

A young American Indian girl named Pocahontas took pity on the settlers. She was the daughter of Chief Powhatan. The Powhatans taught the settlers to hunt, fish, and plant crops.

Jamestown began to grow in size. Smith was wounded in 1609 and had to go back to England. Conditions

New Foods in a New World

The settlers had never seen squash, pumpkins, sunflowers, tomatoes, or corn before. The American Indians taught them how to grow and cook these fruits and vegetables.

John Smith was saved by Pocahontas after his capture by Powhatan's brother. While it is doubtful this rescue actually occurred, it is part of the legend of Pocahontas.

in Jamestown declined. Out of 500 settlers, only 60 survived. Help finally arrived in the spring when Baron De la Warr arrived with more settlers and supplies.

Slavery in the Colonies during the 1700s

This is an advertisement telling colonists in Charlestown that a ship of slaves will be arriving soon, and the slaves will be sold. How would a modern audience respond to an advertisement saying slaves were to be sold in their town? What does this say about the public's attitude about slavery during the 1700s?

A New Crop

By 1614, a man named John Rolfe taught the other settlers to grow a plant called tobacco. The soil and weather conditions were perfect for this crop. It sold for a hefty price in Europe. People began growing tobacco on plantations. New towns were formed, and more people arrived.

Plantation owners needed help in the fields. They began to use indentured servants and slaves as cheap labor.

The House of Burgesses

Landowners in Jamestown formed the House of Burgesses in 1619. This assembly made laws and governed the colony. The elected men represented other members of society. This gave the settlers a voice.

FURTHER EVIDENCE

Slaves kidnapped from Africa did much of the work in many of the colonies. Review Chapter Two. Identify its main point and find supporting evidence. Then visit the Web site below to learn more about the lives of slaves in the New World. Does this information support the main point of Chapter Two? Does it introduce new information?

The African Slave Trade and the Middle Passage
www.pbs.org/wgbh/aia/part1/1narr4.html

CHAPTER THREE

The Colonies of New England

New England colonies included Massachusetts, New Hampshire, Rhode Island, and Connecticut.

The first English settlers to found a colony there were the Puritans. They wanted religious freedom. These 102 settlers arrived at the tip of Cape Cod in September 1620. Their settlement was the first permanent colony in New England.

American Indians hunted deer to bring to the New England colonists. Without help from the American Indians, the colonists might not have survived in their new home.

The Puritans signed an agreement called the Mayflower Compact on board their ship. This document became the first plan to create a government in what would become the United States.

More Settlements

More settlements started around the Massachusetts Bay area. Plymouth, Boston, and other surrounding colonies formed the Massachusetts Bay Colony in 1691. John Smith named the area after the Massachuset American Indian tribe.

America's First College

Boston was founded in 1630. Harvard College was established six years later. It was the first college in the New World. It has since become one of the best institutions of higher learning in the world. Harvard was named in honor of Boston minister John Harvard. In its early years, the college trained Puritan ministers.

Providence Colony

Roger Williams was a Puritan minister living in Boston. In 1636 he bought land from the

Rhode Island colonists welcomed Governor Roger Williams with a colonial charter in 1644.

Narragansett Indians and started Providence Colony in Rhode Island. This colony became a safe haven for people of all religious beliefs.

Connecticut

Minister Thomas Hooker lived near Boston. He and 100 followers decided to move west and begin a new community. They founded the town of Hartford.

Soon several towns sprang up in the new colony of Connecticut.

The settlers sent their governor, John Winthrop II, to England to ask King Charles II for a charter. Charles II granted them the land they had settled, as well as all land stretching west to the Pacific Ocean. This land was occupied by American Indians. No one knew how much land that was.

New Hampshire

New Hampshire started to be settled in 1623. It was part of a large piece of land King James I had given to two friends, John Mason and Ferdinando Gorges. The men divided the land at the Piscataqua River. Gorges took the land east of the river. This would become Maine. Mason took the land west of the river. This was named New Hampshire. It became a separate royal province in 1679.

The Mayflower Compact

William Bradford's book *Of Plymouth Plantation, 1620-1647* has a record of the Mayflower Compact. It is outlined below.

> *Having undertaken, for the glory of God, and advancement of the Christian faith, and honor of our King and Country, a voyage to plant the first colony . . . do by these presents solemnly and mutually, in the presence of God, and one of another, covenant and combine our selves together into a civil body politic, for our better ordering and preservation and furtherance of the ends aforesaid . . . and by virtue hereof to enact, constitute, and frame such just and equal laws, ordinances, acts, constitutions and offices, from time to time, as shall be thought most . . . for the general good of the Colony, unto which we promise all due submission and obedience.*
>
> Source: Bradford, William. Of Plymouth Plantation, 1620–1647. New York: Modern Library, 1967. Print. 75–76.

Consider Your Audience

Review the Mayflower Compact. How might you rewrite it for a different audience, such as your parents or younger friends? Write a blog post conveying this same information for your new audience. What is the best way to get your point across to this audience? How does your new approach differ from the original text? Why?

CHAPTER FOUR

The Middle Atlantic Colonies

The English were not the only Europeans settling in America. The French had colonized present-day Canada. Spanish explorers had settled Florida. The Middle Atlantic colonies of New York, Maryland, Delaware, New Jersey, and Pennsylvania were founded by Dutch and Swedes, as well as the English.

Dutch merchants traded with American Indians on Manhattan Island during the 1600s.

Colony of New York History

Approximately 30 Dutch families settled along the Hudson River in 1624. They called their settlement New Netherland. It was built on the land that is now New York City. In 1625, they began building a town they named New Amsterdam.

The colony of New Sweden was formed in March 1638. This was the only Swedish colony in America. A group of Dutch colonists led by governor Peter Stuyvesant attacked the Swedish settlement in 1655. The Swedish colonists had no choice but to surrender. The Dutch forced the colony to become part of New Netherland.

War broke out between England and the Netherlands in 1664. The Duke of York led English soldiers in capturing all of the Dutch colonies. The

The Purchase of Manhattan Island

Dutch governor Peter Minuit bought Manhattan Island from the Lenape tribe in exchange for cloth, beads, and other goods. The goods were about $500 in today's money.

Peter Stuyvesant surrendered New Netherland to English forces under the Duke of York in 1664.

area was once again renamed. From then on it would be known as New York.

Catholics Find a New Home

Like the Puritans, Roman Catholics sought a new life because they wanted religious freedom. The colony of Maryland would become a safe haven for Roman Catholics in 1634.

Maryland passed a religious toleration act in 1649. This was the first such act in the colonies. It meant people were free to practice any religion they chose, as long as it was a Christian religion.

New Jersey and Delaware

The area once known as New Sweden was divided when the Duke of York took over. Part of the land became the colony of New Jersey. A charter was drafted that allowed freedom of religion, and all men had the right to vote.

The land that became Delaware was a melting pot of European cultures. In addition to English colonists, French, Finnish, Dutch, and Swedish immigrants called it home.

William Penn Founds Pennsylvania

Pennsylvania was given by King Charles II to William Penn. The king owed a large sum of money to Penn's

A statue of William Penn, founder of Pennsylvania, can be seen in Philadelphia.

father. Penn had become a Quaker and wanted to move to America so he could practice his faith freely. In 1681, King Charles gave Penn a piece of land bigger than England. This land became Pennsylvania. Pennsylvania provided a place Quakers could call home. Penn created a plan for the government of his colony.

CHAPTER FIVE

The Southern Colonies

Virginia, North Carolina, South Carolina, and Georgia made up the southern colonies. King Charles I issued a grant for lands south of Virginia in 1624. Farmers and other settlers began to move into the area. Permanent settlements were established during the 1650s.

A grant from King Charles II gave eight English lords the land of Carolina in 1663. These lords were

Spanish forces from Florida battled James Oglethorpe in colonial Georgia in 1742.

called proprietors. They hoped to earn rich profits from crops grown in Carolina. The first permanent settlement was founded in what is now South Carolina by 1670. The area was officially split into North Carolina and South Carolina in 1729. The land was bought back by King Charles II and became royal colonies.

Land of Pirates, Rice, and Indigo

Charles Town (later to be renamed Charleston) was founded in South Carolina in 1680. This busy port became an important city during the 1600s and 1700s. Crops such as rice and

Blackbeard

The legendary Blackbeard is one of history's most famous pirates. The man whose real name was Edward Teach has become part of American folklore. He sailed the waters of the Caribbean Sea and the coasts of Virginia, North Carolina, and South Carolina. He forced some ships to pay tolls. He stole fortunes from others. Many sailors were scared of Blackbeard. He hung smoking pieces of rope from his hat and braided his beard to look like snakes. He was killed by a lieutenant from Virginia in 1718.

The southern colonies of North Carolina and South Carolina were a haven for pirates who raided both settlements and oceangoing ships.

indigo were shipped from Charleston. As in the North, the need for plantation workers led to African slaves being brought to the area. Soon South Carolina had more slaves than free colonists. The plantation owners of South Carolina became very wealthy thanks to this forced labor and the richness of the farmland.

Pirates, who committed crimes on the sea such as robbery, made North Carolina a base for their criminal activities.

Georgia Becomes the Last of the Thirteen Colonies

The last of the original 13 colonies was Georgia. It was founded in 1732 by James Oglethorpe. He had an interesting and noble idea. He founded Georgia as an alternative for prisoners. People who could not pay their debts were sent to prison. Oglethorpe thought these people could be given their own farms in Georgia and work to repay their debts.

Oglethorpe had good intentions, but his plan didn't work. Many prisoners preferred to stay in prison rather than going to the unsettled lands of Georgia. Oglethorpe passed laws that banned owning slaves and drinking alcohol. Most ignored these laws. Still, people began moving into Georgia. It became another British colony in 1752. Oglethorpe was at least successful with one of his plans. He helped to design Savannah, a beautiful city known for its parks and public squares.

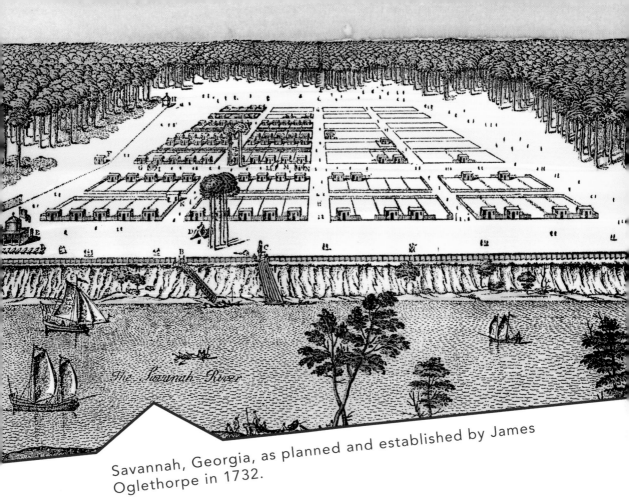

Savannah, Georgia, as planned and established by James Oglethorpe in 1732.

To the south, Georgia bordered Florida, a Spanish colony. Georgians endured much fighting with the Spaniards, who believed the lands of Georgia and the Carolinas actually belonged to Spain. Georgia had its share of trouble with pirates as well.

CHAPTER SIX

The Thirteen Colonies Fight to Become a Nation

The 13 British colonies in America were home to 250,000 European settlers and African slaves by 1700. By 1775, that number had grown to 2.5 million people.

Life in the 13 colonies wasn't easy. The very first settlers had to rely on the land for almost everything. While some colonies were able to become friendly with their American Indian neighbors, bloody conflicts

Before the American Revolution, colonists met to protest British treatment of the colonies.

were a common part of life. Colonists pushed American Indians out of their lands and spread diseases for which the American Indians had no protection.

Many colonists were farmers. Others were fishermen, skilled craftsmen, or merchants. Older and larger towns typically had a flour mill to grind wheat into flour, a general store, a blacksmith, a furniture maker, and a candle maker. Families lived on small farms where they raised animals.

Time for Change

As colonists began to settle beyond the Appalachian Mountains, they faced opposition from the French. France had claimed a large piece of territory between the Mississippi River and the Appalachians. Fighting soon broke out. Some American Indian tribes joined the fighting on both sides. This conflict lasted from 1754 to 1763 and was called the French and Indian War. The British and their colonists finally won in 1763.

The British army was ambushed near Lake George, New York, during the French and Indian War in 1755.

King George III placed taxes on goods shipped to the colonies to help pay for the cost of this war. Colonists had to spend more money for many everyday items. The colonists did not think Great Britain should be able to tax them when they did not have a representative in the British government. The colonists protested the taxes and urged each other not to buy British products. The king responded by increasing taxes even more.

By this time, some of the American

The Boston Tea Party

Colonists were angered by the King of England's taxes on goods such as glass, paper, and tea. They responded by not buying these products. Some colonists decided to take their anger a step further. Led by Samuel Adams, a group of about 60 protestors dressed up as Mohawk American Indians on December 16, 1773. They boarded ships that held imported tea and dumped 342 chests of tea into the harbor. The tea they threw overboard was worth millions of dollars in today's money.

Americans tore down a statue of King George III in New York City to celebrate independence in July 1776.

colonies had been established for more than 100 years. The taxes and restrictions placed on goods only increased their desire for independence.

Revolutionary War Breaks Out

The Revolutionary War between the colonies and Great Britain broke out in 1775. On July 4, 1776, representatives from the 13 colonies met in Philadelphia to create the Declaration of Independence. This document said the 13 colonies were now their own country.

Of course Great Britain would not simply allow the colonies to declare their independence. The Revolutionary War continued until 1783. After eight years of bloodshed, the colonies became the first 13 states of the new United States of America.

The Declaration of Independence

Thomas Jefferson wrote the document called the Declaration of Independence in 1776. It stated the 13 colonies were now independent from Great Britain.

> When in the Course of human events, it becomes necessary for one people to dissolve the political bands which have connected them with another, and to assume among the powers of the earth, the separate and equal station to which the Laws of Nature and of Nature's God entitle them, a decent respect to the opinions of mankind requires that they should declare the causes which impel them to the separation. . . . these United Colonies are, and of Right ought to be Free and Independent States.
>
> Source: "Declaration of Independence." The National Archives. July 4, 1776. Web. http://www.archives.gov/exhibits/charters/declaration_transcript.html.

Changing Minds

The Declaration of Independence discusses the reasons the Founding Fathers believed the colonies should be free of Great Britain's rule. Take a position on this belief. Imagine your best friend has the opposite opinion. Write a short essay trying to change your friend's mind. Make sure you state your opinion and your reasons for it. Include facts and details that support your reasons.

IMPORTANT DATES

1585

First attempt to begin an English colony at Roanoke Island.

1607

Jamestown Colony is successfully established.

1620

Puritans leave England and arrive in Plymouth, Massachusetts, in September.

1636

Roger Williams flees Boston and founds Providence, Rhode Island.

1638

Swedish settlers found New Sweden.

1663

South Carolina is chartered.

1623

New Hampshire starts to be settled.

1624

New Netherland is established by the Dutch.

1634

Maryland is settled by a group of Catholics.

1681

William Penn founds Pennsylvania.

1729

North Carolina and South Carolina are officially split into two colonies.

1732

Georgia is founded by James Oglethorpe.

STOP AND THINK

Say What?

Find five words in this book you've never seen or heard before. Find out what these words mean. Write the meaning of each word in your own words. Once you're finished, use each word in a new sentence.

Why Do I Care?

Come up with two or three ways the subject of this book connects to your life. For example, did you ever try to do something new and frightening in order to get something important to you, as the colonists did when they moved to the New World? How did you overcome the obstacles? In the end, were you glad to have faced the challenge?

You Are There

Imagine you live during colonial days in America. Write 300 words describing your life. What do you see happening in your settlement? What kinds of things do you eat every day? What are your siblings doing?

Tell the Tale

This book discusses how the American Indians were pushed off their land by European settlers and how some of them reacted to this. While some colonists and tribes were hostile to one another, others became allies. Write 200 words that tell the true story of a American Indian or a tribe that came to the aid of the settlers. Be sure to set the scene, develop a sequence of events, and offer a conclusion.

GLOSSARY

assembly
a group of people who make and agree upon laws

blacksmith
a person who repairs or makes objects from metal

charter
written permission granting certain rights

indigo
a plant grown in warm climates used to make blue dye

merchant
a shopkeeper or a person who buys and sells goods

plantation
a large farm worked by servants or slaves who live there

port
a city with a harbor where large ships can anchor

proprietor
a person granted ownership of a colony and given permission to establish laws and sell the land

religious toleration
to be accepting of religious beliefs other than one's own

LEARN MORE

Books

Britton, Tamara. *The Georgia Colony*. Edina: ABDO Publishing, 2001. Print.

Gray, Edward G. *Colonial America: A History in Documents*. New York: Oxford University Press, 2003. Print.

Hakim, Joy. *Making Thirteen Colonies: 1600–1740*. New York: Oxford University Press, 2003.

Web Links

To learn more about the 13 colonies, visit ABDO Publishing Company online at **www.abdopublishing.com**. Web sites about the 13 colonies are featured on our Book Links page. These links are routinely monitored and updated to provide the most current information available. Visit **www.mycorelibrary.com** for free additional tools for teachers and students.

INDEX

ABOUT THE AUTHOR

Susan E. Hamen lives in Minnesota with her husband, daughter, and son. She has written 14 books for children and loves researching and learning about new topics with every book she writes.